Sometimes I Like to Be Alone

Also by Heidi Goennel:
Seasons
When I Grow Up . . .
My Day
If I Were a Penguin . . .

Illustrated by Heidi Goennel:
in Just- spring **by E. E. Cummings**

Sometimes I Like to Be Alone

Heidi Goennel

Little, Brown and Company
Boston   Toronto   London

First edition

Library of Congress Cataloging-in-Publication Data

Goennel, Heidi.
     Sometimes I like to be alone/Heidi Goennel.
          p.   cm.
     Summary: Text and illustrations describe
some of the special things that one can do alone.
     ISBN 0-316-31842-6 (lib. bdg.)
     [1. Solitude—Fiction.]   I. Title.
PZ7.G554So 1989
[E]—dc19   88-30780
                                                       CIP
                                                        AC

                    10 9 8 7 6 5 4 3 2 1

Published simultaneously in Canada
by Little, Brown & Company (Canada) Limited

Printed in Italy

To Peter

Sometimes I like to be alone.
There are lots of things I can
do all by myself.

When I'm alone, I like to
dance to my favorite song
and pretend I'm in a chorus line.

When I'm alone, I like to
decorate a cake
for my mommy as
a big surprise.

When I'm alone, I like to watch my favorite movie and eat lots of popcorn.

When I'm alone, I like to paint a big picture on an easel — just like a real artist.

When I'm alone, I like to try on grown-up clothes and act like a pretty lady.

When I'm alone, I like to
make a special card
to send to my friend who
lives far away.

When I'm alone, I like to go fishing and try to catch my own dinner.

When I'm alone, I like to
sit in Daddy's special place
and read stories and poems.

When I'm alone, I like to teach my puppy new tricks.

When I'm alone, I like to
look out my bedroom window
and watch for shooting stars.

When I'm alone, I like to work on a jigsaw puzzle and do all the edges first.

When I'm alone, I like to sneak downstairs on Christmas Eve and listen for reindeer.

When I'm alone, I sometimes
just like to think about things
or maybe do nothing at all.